First published in 2018 by Quadrille Publishing
Copyright © 2018 Quadrille Publishing | quadrille.com
Quadrille is an imprint of Hardie Grant | hardiegrant.com
Design: The Studio of Williamson Curran (TSOWC)
978 1 78713 220 7
Printed in China